The Man from Misery
and Other Poems

Brandon Hodge

iUniverse, Inc.
New York   Bloomington

The Man from Misery and Other Poems

The following is an extension of the copyright page "Isn't It Funny" appeared in Honey of the Soul (Page 228) published by the International Library of Poetry, 2003; "Wedding Bellbottom Blues" appeared in the International Who's Who in Poetry published by the International Library of Poetry, 2004; "Temperamental" appeared in Colours of the Heart published by Noble House Publishers, 2004; "What I've Done" appeared in Tracing the Infinite published by the International Library of Poetry, 2004; "Reflections of my Fall" appeared in Labours of Love published by Noble House Publishers, 2005; "Pedestrian" and "Ode to the Green Grass" since retitled "Salute to the Green Grass" appeared in Image: The Literary Magazine of WVU Tech (pages 20, 50) published by the English department of WVU Tech, May 2008; "The Girl in the band room" and "Waiting" appeared in Image: The Literary Magazine of WVU Tech (pages 4, 11) published by the English department of WVU Tech, May 2009.

iUniverse books may be ordered through booksellers or by contacting:

iUniverse
1663 Liberty Drive
Bloomington, IN 47403
www.iuniverse.com
1-800-Authors (1-800-288-4677)

ISBN: 978-1-4502-5080-1 (sc)
ISBN: 978-1-4502-5079-5 (dj)
ISBN: 978-1-4502-5078-8 (ebook)

Library of Congress Control Number: 2010911833

Printed in the United States of America

iUniverse rev. date: 08/03/10

For Mamaw B., Papaw J., and Sammie, I love and miss you all. And for Mr. Poe, thank you very much.

Words won't stop coming;

like a poetry fountain,

as many poems as high as a mountain.

INTRODUCTION

Life is melancholy. It's an odyssey of pain and self-discovery; artists like myself know this better than most—Poe knew it; Plath knew it; and I know it. We artists are all victims of our own gifts; they make us what we are and simultaneously take it away. My name is Brandon Hodge, and I wrote this book.

You're likely asking yourself why you should buy and/or read this poetry from a poet you have never heard of. The answer is actually quite simple, although it may take some explanation. First and foremost, you should read this book because I wrote it for you, not for fame or for money, but for you and anyone who has ever been different. By one doctor's expert opinion, I shouldn't even be here, but for some other reasons that I have yet to figure out, I am still alive. I have survived autoimmune disease, lung cancer, and depression, among other things. I've witnessed death after death of relatives and friends and taken each one so personally. I've lost the love of my life to my own demons. I've been witness to much deception and betrayal within my own family and from others. It is only the love of words that's kept me going; in writing I've found comfort.

I, like many, found writing at any early age—as early as third grade or maybe earlier. I was writing short stories on notebook paper, just kids stories in shabby handwriting. I'm sure there are many children who do that sort of thing. Mine were usually one to two or maybe three pages front and back; nothing special. What is special is that most children do other things; they grow out of it, whatever you call it. I kept doing it. I like to think they got progressively better, like my poetry, although it was years before I realized the significance of it.

In 1997, I was eleven years old. That year in literature class, we were given an assignment to write a poem. My poem was "The Murder," and it is the first poem in this book. I thought it appropriate. That was also the year I wrote my most beloved short story called "Ed's Odyssey." It's never been published and likely never will be; it's a relatively simple story about a cat and a hobo and their odyssey through a small section of New York one summer day in 1977. It, too, was written by hand on notebook paper. All of my poems and short stories are written by hand; a computer screen is not a blank canvas, at least not for me. Some time later, I wrote a long sequel called "Ed's Exodus," and I think it safe to say it surpassed the original.

There is a gap in this book between 1997 and 2002. Don't mistake that for a dormant period; I did write in those years, just not anything worthy. My poetry seems to be triggered by heightened emotional states; the stronger the emotions, whether they are lust, anger, or joy, the better and easier it is for me to write. When I am emotional, writing is as easy as breathing. In recent years, I have learned how to tap into my writing so that I don't have to be distraught or in a heightened emotional state in order to write, although it does require more effort.

You might find yourself asking why some of my poems are so cryptic and why I write this way. Who are those girls of whom I speak, Sam, Sammie, Karyla? I really can't explain why they might seem cryptic; it's just my style. You should know that most of these poems were written when I was under extreme emotional duress. In truth, I'm a very lonely person. I wrote this book for people like me—people who have been told they're different, people who are different, anyone who has ever been so lonely it made their chest hurt, anyone who has ever been so racked with sorrow and regret that they couldn't get out of bed, people like me. I'll be honest: I'm hoping to God that this book opens doors for me, that it will lead to something better, to new people, to places I've literally never been. My dreams are to write and travel, to drive from place to place, to do book signings, and things like that. It's all I've ever wanted for myself: simplicity. I'm a loner, and that should be obvious by now. People like me don't fit in with normal folk; normal folk don't write like me. I don't do anything normal, and most folk have certain ideas about what a poet is supposed to be like, stereotypes if you will: the strange and reclusive poet with the weird hairdo and black clothes, the unconventional sort. I've not had much contact with others of my kind, so I don't know if that's what most poets are like today, but that goes back to why you should read me: because I am like that. I'm not Goth, but I do wear black. I live alone; I do everything alone. I'm plagued by personal demons. I'm quiet. I have a mop top of curly and unkempt hair. And most of all, I'm sensitive and truly lost most of the time. I don't know the rules concerning that kind of thing, like if you know you are lost, then you really aren't, or if it's like alcoholism, you are and you just have to admit you have a problem.

Let me assure you, I have problems. If you want your poet to be mostly miserable and Poe-like, look no further. I do lack a few poetic stereotypes though—I'm not an alcoholic; I don't indulge in drugs, whether that be opium or absinthe; the green fairy is not after my soul. I have had some unhappy love affairs, although I don't know if I would call them torrid. I've made enemies; every artist is entitled to piss some people off, just like they're entitled to go to Paris once before they die, which I have not done yet but I am hopeful that I'll get my chance. I've never attempted suicide like some writers have, but when you've come as close to death as I have, you gain an appreciation for life, no matter how dreary it may seem. I'm dead set on living. I'm still looking for my own personal lost Lenore, although it seems less and less likely that I am going to find her, but maybe it's like I said: I've already found her and lost her to my own personal demons, in which case she truly is lost. I won't tell you her name, she wouldn't want me to, but there are a great many poems about her in this book. Try and guess which one she is.

Perhaps I've talked about myself enough for you to know I'm the real deal; that I'm a real poet, not a fame seeker or money grubber. I may be a hack, I'm sure some will say so, but I won't steer you wrong. My poems are real, and I plan on writing them for a long time to come, so I hope you stick with me. It would be nice to have a fan or two.

But enough about me; let me talk to you about the book. One of the great things I love about poetry is anonymity, not of person but of meaning. The poems are written for anyone who wants to read them, and I hope that everyone who reads them takes something away from them. If I inspired you or made you think, made you stop and say "wow," or even "what the hell," then I've succeeded. Poetry evokes or awakens the nobler and higher emotions. I was emotional when I wrote most of these, perhaps that emotion can be felt by the reader, like a literary earthquake felt far, far away. A few things I would like to point out are: Sam and Sammie are two different people. They live in different places and they've never met, as far as I know, but they both have a special place in my heart, as do all the others. I think a true student of poetry can find inspiration anywhere in anything, even when he isn't looking for it. Everything is a poem waiting to be written, a painting waiting to be painted, or a song waiting to be sung. Not everyone can see it, and that's what separates artists from ordinary folk.

Some of these poems have a sexual undertone. Not all of them were intentional, they just came out that way. I don't want to explain those poems; I would rather you read them and make your own interpretation. I hope you agree as you read this book that the poems get progressively better as the years move forward. I'm sure some will disagree with that statement. There are always critics; you can't grow as an artist without them. I don't handle criticism well, but I'm not naïve. I can't do something like this and not be judged, so I'll take the critique as best I can. I just hope those critics have an open mind. That's really what it takes to appreciate any kind of art; it's all subjective, one man's masterpiece is another man's firewood. I'm sure I'll catch flack for the poems that don't rhyme. I can say in my own defense that poetry isn't about rhyme, it's about meaning. Although I'm sure that statement won't help either. I'm not good with meter and that kind of thing, although I am working on it. Great artists are always trying new things, and I will expand my style and get better; you just have to bear with me. I advocate free verse, because I'm a nonconformist, I don't like confining rules, and I'm just not very good at writing in other styles, not yet.

There are a few poems, such as "Samuel," addressed to and/or about my son. I'll be forthright—I don't have a son. You can call those fiction if you choose, or perhaps just poems written in advance. I like to think of the son in those poems as anybody's son, even though his name may not be Samuel; although I'm sure someone out there has a son with that name, and, hey, maybe I'll gain some popularity and someone will read that poem and name their son that in honor of me; wishful thinking. The poems where the child has no name, such as "Oh, Baby," well that's anyone's baby. Print that poem, frame it, put it on your wall; the person I wrote it for did. Some of these poems have Latin words in them. They are for poetic effect; that and they just sound better. Examples are words such as inamorata, that just means the feminine of the word beloved; if your beloved is a man, then it's inamorato. Don't be intimidated by those Latin words. I just used a thesaurus.

A lot of these poems are untitled. I apologize for that, but when I am scribbling poems faster than my brain can process them, I don't find much time for titles. Some people will know what I mean, but for those of you who don't look at the poem "Papaw" (that's my grandfather in case you don't know what the word means, likewise my grandmother is Mamaw). They're both gone now. I'll tell you about them because it's relevant to my purpose. My grandmother on my mom's side died in 2008. I loved her very much. Hers is one of those deaths I mentioned that I take very personally. She really supported my writing. The first time I read aloud to a crowd was in 2008, not long before she died. She was able to come and listen to me, and that meant a lot. My papaw, her husband, died in 1989 when I was four years old. I don't remember him much, just flashes really. I've grown up hearing about him; he's sort of become the yardstick to which I am measuring myself in this world. He's become almost mythical to me. It's been so long and I've thought about him so much that sometimes in my solitude I find myself wondering if he ever really existed at all or if I just dreamt him up. Being diagnosed as having depression and being a loner means sometimes things tend to get blurry; the line between the real and the dream is hazy, like waking up and not being completely awake. God knows I don't feel that way all the time, but sometimes on those days a lot of things enter my mind, like if anything is real or if it is all a dream. Am I going to suddenly wake up and discover that I'm still five years old, still sleeping on those Ninja Turtle bed sheets? It's in thinking like that that great poetry can be found.

I foresee two things coming from the reading of this introduction: either you will sympathize with me and possibly read my work, or you will say I'm nuts, in which case you probably won't read my work. Either way, I hope you take something from this book; that alone will make the writing well worth it. I hope you enjoy this book. I once said to myself that this book is my *Tamerlane,* my very own *Leaves of Grass.* I don't expect you will feel quite as much, but again, wishful thinking.

Brandon Hodge

Contents

2004

2005

2006

2007

2008

2009

1997

This was the year I discovered poetry. I wrote my first poem, "The Murder," in seventh grade literature class as an assignment. I was eleven years old, and I don't remember the grade I received for it.

The Murder

The murder made you stutter.
The body was in the gutter.
The head cut off,
All safety lost.
The blood was in the drain.
The sound echoes in your brain.
The eyes create many whys,
As you say your last good-byes.

2002

Unreachable

So clearly I see that love is denied to us,
Unreachable for you and me.
Haunted by the ghosts of love attempts past,
And now our empty existence fills with sorrow
So fast.
The love we sought before
Mourns us evermore.
And although it hurts us so,
We go on after that love
To happier places.
That's where we go.
So clearly I see that love is denied to us,
Unreachable for you and me.
But in that place love takes us to,
You know that's where I will always love you.

Sam

My blonde beauty, how I loved you,
Your eyes deep and cool water blue.
I miss you every day.

My blonde beauty, your smile is so beautiful.
And I miss you so much.
And how I long for your touch.

My blonde beauty, I can still feel you,
Your kiss upon my lips,
And your warm cheek against mine.

My blonde beauty, with hair flowing long,
So warm, so soft.

My blonde beauty, your name spoken is worth
Everything I have in the world.
Without you I have already lost everything.

My blonde beauty, I prize you above all things.

Although you are gone,
I hear your voice in my dreams.
I see your face next to me on my pillow.
You are all that I am.
I love you always,
Always and forever, my Sam.

Isn't It Funny

Isn't it funny how simplistic love looks
And how difficult it really is?
Simple for everyone else but hard for you.

Isn't it funny what you'll do
To win the object of your affection,
Although you know your efforts are pointless?

Isn't it funny how wrong the person your love chooses is for them and how
obvious it is?

Isn't it funny how you always fall in love
With the people that hate you the most?

Isn't it funny what you think,
What you'll do,
And what you'll break?

Isn't it funny
What you'll do for that moment of clarity?
Isn't it funny?

My Blood

My blood is thick and ageless, flowing endlessly
Through arteries and veins that never end.
My blood is spilled upon the ground where we met,
Where we walked, where we loved.
My blood is yours to save your life.
My blood upon your hands is the sacrifice,
The sacrifice I make for love.
My blood escapes me here where I lay,
Where I look into your eyes.
My blood flows to more than distant earth,
Into the soul of a child that as I die
Shall through you … live.

My blood is gone but you're still here.
So is my child living by blood once belonged to me,
Spilled upon the ground where we met,
Where we walked, where we loved.

Eyes of Adoration

When I look into the mirror, I see two faces;
One is mine and the other is yours.
But you are not really there.
I know I hear your voice in the dark.
I swear I feel your touch in my sleep.

When I look into the mirror, I see two figures;
In the haunted reflection before me,
Eyes of adoration long past.

When I look into the mirror, I hear a voice
That I once knew, and I feel a presence all around me.
When I breathe deep it's your sweet scent that I smell.
In my dreams it's your sweet face I see,
And your touch that I feel.

What I've Done

What I've done,
What I am doing,
What I will do,
Every day I ask myself.
When will I be free? When will I find someone?
When it's all over and done?

What I have done,
Given my heart to more girls than one,
But still I am alone.

What I am doing,
Searching for another soul tonight,
But try as I might I am still sad this night.

What will I do?
I will keep searching for her,
And one day when I have worn holes in my feet,
My love and I will meet.

That Fire in You

You are my love and my heart,
And a fire burns in your eyes.
A fire I can't explain, but it's there
Just the same.

A fire burns in your heart for someone,
someone who burns for you.

You are my love and my beloved.
Your fire burns deep as does mine.
Don't lose that fire.
My heart would burn out too,

If I'm forced to live without you.

This Life of Mine

I renew my objection
To this pointless endeavor,
A life spent searching for something better.
And irony is seen, for you see,
My endeavor is but my own pointless life,
And a happy life is taking forever.

The Man from Misery

I am the voice of sorrow,
And it echoes even now.
After the life I had is gone,
And my reasons for sorrow have left me.

I loved a girl who loved someone else,
Someone who wasn't me.
And for all those days I tried to get her back,
I failed.

Now I am alone and with regret.
I am closed to the world
And with insecurities beset.

I loved the girl named Sam,
But it's all past.
What became of Sam
I do not know.

It was misery trying to win her back,
But that place I went.
I took her with me.

Sorrow besets me now.
Thoughts of love haunt me to the core.
And all that I was went with Sam,
Left me what I am.

Alone and bitter cold,
The man from sorrow sprung.
The man from misery.

Oh, Baby

Baby, Baby, in the crib,
The morning sun rises for you.
Don't cry.
You're not all alone,
And you never will be.
You're loved by a great many
For your little fingers,
Your bright eyes,
And the joy you bring into our world.

Baby, Baby, in the crib,
The hour which life begins
Begins to take it away.
Don't be afraid,
Because mom and dad love you,
And all the cute baby things,
The cute baby things that you do.
You're cute as a button and a joy.
You're our special, little boy.

Baby, Baby, in the crib,
You'll have wonderful memories.
Memories to smile about;
Food on your bib,
Cheerios in mommy's hair.
You'll laugh and cry,
But you'll always be,
Mommy and daddy's special little guy.

Baby, Baby, in the crib,
You're such a wonderful way for a life a life to begin.
And now it's time to sleep,
So close your eyes,
Start to yawn, dream until the dawn.

In My Dreams

My dreams speak of black waterfalls and dark skies,
Of nighttime waters flowing deep.

My dreams speak of silence, quiet as the grave,
The smell,
The smell of roses rotting on the cold, cold ground.

My dreams speak of unspeakable things,
That which I fear
In the darkness of the night.

My dreams speak of dark places and of eyes,
Eyes that only I see.

My dreams speak of loss, pain, and sorrow,
And of strangers,
Strangers who walk in shadows behind us.

My dreams speak of dreams that frighten me,
Things that whisper.
Dreams I may dream again.

2003

Sweet Lilley That Shines

Sweet Lilley that shines, you are fragrant
And beautiful in my garden by the door.

Sweet Lilley that shines,
Your beauty may wilt in time.
But whether roses or ashes,
I'll never forget your return in the spring.
And to my heart you do a marvelous thing.

I Know about Her

I know about her, that girl that's alone,
Standing by the door.
I know her fears and much, much more.

I know about her, that girl that's quiet,
Searching for a man to give her adore.
I know her likes: cats, circuses, and soup.

I know about her, that girl that's outcasted.
She feels like no one cares at all.
I know her dislikes: clowns
And the ocean but not the beach.

I know about her, that girl possessing hair,
Hair with streaks of red.
She writes when she feels bad,
And she cries out her beautiful brown eyes
When she is sad.

I know about her.

Poem Number 72

Today I am inspired,
Inspired by hopes of romance and possibility.
What a glorious feeling to anticipate the unexpected.

Today I am inspired,
Inspired to write great things about subjects,
Subjects I can't understand,
To look for what I have never seen.

Today I am inspired.
She inspired the creativity in me,
Stirred the inner emotion,
Set free the life that is in me.
Today I am inspired.

For Lindsey

The days of connection between us have passed away.
All I have to say is just for Lindsey.
I speak with words from my lonely heart.
And all I desire to be lonely no more is you.

I believe in angels, and all I have to say is this:
I know what you are.
I know where you came from.
You're an angel in my eyes,
A heavenly song on the sunrise.

The days of connection between us belong to you and I.
And always your gorgeous eyes shine bright and I see poetry.

Athena, would you make me happy?
I'll make you smile and laugh a while,
And you'll know all the love I have is for you.

All the love I have is for Lindsey. I would do anything,
Everything to win your gentle embrace, your respect, your whimsy.

I would do anything and everything to make you happy,
Even write a poem that's really sappy.
I did it all for Lindsey.

Lindsey Angel

Love will last forever,
Into realms beyond time.
Now as I write this rhyme,
Deep within me, feelings stir.
So many there are inside,
Every dream, every thought
Yearns to be explored.
But always they end the same,
Next to no one, I stand alone.
Give me your love, you already have mine.
Everything I do or see reminds me of you.
Let me in, Lindsey Angel, and we can fly away.

That Tender Moment

I remember the nights we spent by the fire
Under a blanket together.
I kissed your lips and held you in desire.

Outside snow began to fall,
And all I could see was you close to me.

Unaffected by time, lost in a tender moment.

I remember the nights we spent by the fire
Under a blanket together.
I kissed your lips and held you in desire,

For that tender moment.

Temperamental

I am temperamental today.
I lash out in spite of tranquility.
I am blinded by vengeful vengeance,
Consumed by violent violence.
I am temperamental today.

I was temperamental yesterday.
I screamed to the heavens above.
I kicked the dirt below,
And hurt those that I know.
I was temperamental yesterday.

I will be temperamental tomorrow.
I am always the angry soul with blood-boiling sorrow raging.
My eyes wide open and searching for a fight,
My invitation open to anyone
and everyone that crosses me that night.

I will be temperamental tomorrow.

Pacific Isle

The sun rises over the morning fog by the sea.
My ship waits for me.

Today I will sail away,
But will always remember this day.

For love I must go and leave her side.
How I will suffer, and how she will cry.

Love is too precious to watch sail away.
Don't leave without me, not today.

We will leave together,
Chance the unknown weather.
Say farewell to family and friends,
This is where their part of the story ends.

Away with the morning sun,
Our journey has just begun.

Somewhere in Time

Climb aboard, Lindsey Angel.
It's time to go.
Say your final farewells to family and friends.
We will never see them again
How it hurts you, honey,
No one feels it more than I

Our vessel is ready. If we stay here,
Our lives are doomed.
This life on earth is over for all
But you and I.
I want to take you with me,
To where the universe may begin again.

Good-bye earth,
Summer breezes, and memories. Lindsey will survive
And pass through to the next world.

Our children will see earth
Only in pictures;
But will never grow old
And will never die,
But start a new world somewhere in time.

Whatever lay beyond the stars, we will find together.
We are the only,
And our children will come to know this day.
I am Adam as you are Eve.
So cry, Lindsey angel,
But never forget you will always have me.

Somewhere in time.

What I Know Now

What I know now:
I know sorrow and regret,
Love and poetry.
I know no reason for which I am
Imprisoned in hatred.

What I know now:
I know love unbroken is shattered,
Shattered on the floor.
Who knocks on my door when demons come?
I know no reason
Why love had to give up and die.

What I know now:
I know poetry; only in anger does it flow.
What vengeance do I crave?
I know no reason for what I know now.

I know … I'll always know.

The Mad House

Here in the mad house
Houses the depraved and the insane,
Driven by demons,
Condemned by men.

Shut away in darkness.
But what is dark
To those with eyes of black
And souls ill with evil?

What is evil
To those in the mad house,
Those at home in pain and suffering,
Driven by demons,
Condemned by men,

Shut away in darkness?

Heartbreaker

Get away from her; she's my girl,
My love, and my life.

If you touch her,
I will make you cry.

If you say bad things to her,
I'll do worse things to you.

If you steal her heart,
I'll tear you apart.

If you kiss her,
I'll kill you.

If you love her,
I'll never forgive you.

If she loves you,
I'll never understand.

Get away from her.
She'll break my heart.

Two Lovers

Like travelers in the fall breeze, the leaves blow away,
Upward toward the setting sun,

To those two lovers in each others arms,
Music on the sunset and love in their hearts.

For those two lovers
Begins a never-ending journey
Across the vast blue sky.

Because of those two lovers,
A better world it was for her and he.

The fall breeze blow those leaves in the autumn sky,
Past the house where they lived,

The ground where they walked,
To the graves where they lay.

One More Night

All my dreams I have found,
I have found here.
I should have taken a picture, frozen time.
I cry and cry all night, all day.

I can't live without you.
I wanted to dance in the rain,
And kiss you so deep, but it's you I couldn't keep.

The guitar hums, and your voice I can still hear.
This is my last dream.
I dream about one more night.

One more night is all I need to make you see.
Here I go.
Oh, god, I love you so.

Come and go with me
For one more night,
Before you board that flight.

Oh, god, this hurts me so.
Please don't go. Give me one more night,
One more night to make everything right.

Give me one more night.

Nothing Inspires Me

Nothing inspires me to write poetry,
No words from out of the blue,
No verse, but it gets worse.

Nothing inspires me to write poetry,
No rhymes, no thrill, no thought,
Nor the idea of my poetry being bought.

Nothing inspires me to write poetry,
No people, no song,
But hey I'm writing a poem now.

So I guess I was wrong.

About Me

What can be said about me?
How can I write poetry the way that I do if I'm not sad?
My poetry springs from sorrow and pain like all other artists had.

What can be said about me?
I feel things like no other person because I am an artist.
My art springs from my soul like all other artists did.

What can be said about me?
I am who I am and can't be something that I am not.
I am the embodiment of sorrow like all other artists were.

What can be said about me?
I like to push the metaphorical envelope a little too far.
I am an outsider like all other artists are.

What can be said about me?
The strangest things are those that I seek; I am thought by some as a freak.
I am different but not weak; I can be tough like all other artists can.

What can be said about me?
I have walked the places between here and there to come back with rhyme.
In my words I have gone beyond, like all other artists do.

What can be said about me?
I dream of love everlasting that stretches beyond eternity.
I have only found doomed love like all other artists will.

What can be said about me?
My poetry doesn't always rhyme, nor mean what you think.
My words are unique and I wrote them in blood like all other artists should.

What can be said about me?
My soul is deep like the oceans so dark.
Now this poem is nearly done and for all other artists like me I hope you see,
I am the spirit of regret like all other artists feel.

Reflections of My Fall

What have I to learn from?
Am I doomed to a life of loss,
Sorrow for lost love and failed tests?

Many loves walk my mile,
And they never glance.

I am alone.
The leaves are falling.

Fall is my season,
My season for reflection.

Always lonely and bitter,
As fall becomes winter and snowflakes fall,
Fall from the heavens above me.

Time passes by me, and I am powerless.
So bless the autumn trees, leaves,
and the scarecrows in the field.

I Didn't Expect You

I didn't expect you to come into my life,
To complicate things.

I didn't expect you to be so beautiful,
To take focus out of my eyes.

I am fixed on you.
I didn't expect to fall in love.

2004

Mice

Mice, what fascinating creatures you are.
Always up to run and hide.
Eating, sleeping, scurry and run, little mice.
What fascinating creatures you are.

The Sad News

I love you more than anyone ever will.
But that isn't enough.
Why does it always have to be so tough?

I don't make you happy.
And you deserve to be and now it's all I see,
This sorrow that's come between you and me.

The end is fast approaching, and I am afraid.
What will I do without you?
Where will I go?
Will I ever be the same?

I am the barer of unconventional sadness.
You're better off without me.
This is the sad news that I bring you.
What am I to do now?

I hope you find someone who loves you like I do,
And who makes you happy like I don't.

I Speculate

I speculate the reasons you are late.
You were with another on a date.
You choose not to love me anymore.
You refused to enter my open door.
I have wronged you somehow,
For that you hate me now.
I speculate the reasons you are late.
You have found a new love,
By a simple twist of fate.

Malice

What makes you this way,
Cruel and inhumane?
What pain do you possess to inflict harm every day,
Beat the children, kill the dog?
Where do you hide to commit such terrible things,
And not be eaten away inside?

Baby Boy

Never could I be so lucky before now,
Blessed by god somehow.
To smile upon my baby boy,
To hold him here.
Is there life beyond this joy,
Beyond my son, the better part of me?
And it's easy to see,
He won't be the only one.

Fancy

I have an insightful imagination,
Leading me onward
Toward a brighter destination.
Colorful flights of fancy take me away,
Far from here to clear skies,
Where I can play.

A Messed Up World

It's a messed up world,
And it's getting ever worse.
The things I loved are forgotten and gone.
People I cared about,
Dear Heather, taken away in handcuffs.
And her bubble finally burst.

Incubus

A crypt is a sacred place where dead sleep,
No longer bound to earthly feet;
Released from the pain of living;
Bereft of life;
Inanimate and inert.

A poet's crypt brings no rest,
Only death to the tormentors;
Tormentors who haunted the poet in life.
He brings to them horror in their night slumber.

I am the ghost of a poet past,
Returned from beyond
To spread the music of agony
To torture the torturers.

I am not what you think.
I am a nightmare,
A shadow in your dark corner,
A sound in your cellar.

I am the demon spirit of a poet past.

I am the incubus.

Self-assured

I am self-assured and confident here,
Here among the memories of old time.

Side by side along with my love,
The sea flowing nearby,
The tide carrying us away.

Home vanishes into the distance.
Here we are soothed by the rocking,
The rocking of the sea.

Carry us away from home,
To safer places beyond the horizon.

Places where death and sorrow
Cannot follow.

Snowflake

From the glistening sky falls a purest creation,
One unlike any other as they all are.
To the ground it makes pure white.
Never was there anything as beautiful,
As the snowflake falling this night.

The Laughing Snake

Snake in the grass,
He moves with slow style and class.
And before a terrible strike,
He pokes out his forked tongue.
And in his own way pokes his own fun.
Hiss, hiss, hiss

Drive

I love to drive my car,
To places near and far.
I love the wind in my hair.
I love the smell of open-road air.
My life knows no greater thrill
Than being behind the wheel.

Wedding Bellbottom Blues

Saved from a lifetime of loneliness,
Delivered to a lifetime of confusion,
A marriage to a girl I hardly know
Brought on by sex, drugs,
And rock and roll.

The decadent disco era,
I danced, I drank, and I romanced.
I married a stripper in bellbottom pants.

I am at the altar so confused.
I have the wedding bellbottom blues.

The wedding bellbottom blues,
Caused by drugs and bad booze,
Bright lights and platform shoes.

I got no chance.
I got everything to lose.
I got the wedding bellbottom blues.

Untitled

You must love someone else,
The lover better than me.
He doesn't love you more than I.

I may make you cry,
But the lover isn't for you willing to die.

He isn't me.

The Strains of Heavy Metal

I am in a smoke-filled room,
Blind to how I came
Or where I am.

I am choking to death,
The strains of heavy metal on my lungs.

Drug-addled stoners are head-banging me,
Head-banging me to my grave.
And there is no escape.

Let me out of this hell.
Oh well, I can find no freedom now.

Condemnation is my destination.

Five Senses Too Late

My eyes have been stolen,
Taken from my face,
Whisked away to some distant place.

The deceit I cannot see.

My ears fell off,
Fallen to the ground.
Hear I cannot a whisper or a sound.

The lies I cannot hear.

My tongue I have swallowed.
Esophagus it followed.
Tasted I have, my own stomach.

The bitterness of sorrow, I cannot taste.

My nose ran away I suppose,
Gone where smells are plenty,
Gone wherever a nose goes.

I cannot smell what has no scent.

My life ran out of rhyme,
Out of time.
Feel I cannot, the inside of this coffin.

Justice

I am not your judge and jury.

But because of your crime,

Let justice be swift and in a hurry.

Find Me

Find me here, lonely and weeping.

Find me there, joyous and singing.

Find me everywhere, deceiving.

The Forbidden

I am forbidden from what I do,
My movies, money, even you.

I am forbidden to go outside,
To see life from the window's other side.

I am forbidden to live life
The way others do.

I am forbidden to be free
Because of you.

My Cat

My cat prowls the night
With strength and all a cat's might.

My cat will always find food,
Never to suffer a poor human's plight.

My cat is orange like the fires of daylight,
But always in his heart, a creature of the night.

My cat may find itself in another cat fight,
But he will never fall to another's bite.

My cat hunts the night away,
By morning sleeping next to me,
Purrs with delight.

My cat is a predator when comes the night,
But sleeps contently on my floor in the hours before.

Samuel

Samuel, my son,
Your task is far from done.
You are yet to explore life.

Samuel, my son,
You are my only,
My everyone.

Samuel, my son,
Never was a father prouder.

Samuel, my son,
I have always dreamed of you.

Samuel, my son,
I have always believed,

One day you might finally be conceived.

Allegations

They blame me for everything,
All that is wrong in their lives.

I have done nothing,
Still I face accusations and citations.

Why do they yell and scream lies about me,
I cannot see.

Socks

Don't eat my socks.
I don't have many left.

Don't run away under the bed where I can't see.

Don't take your pleasure from biting me.

But always be glad and wag your tail with glee.

Never run into the road where I cannot follow.

Always be loyal.

Don't eat my socks.
I don't have many left.

The Blocked and the Memories

I tried to block her number,
So I could let her go.
She found another way to call,
And now I see it all.

I tried to forget her memories,
Her smile and her face.
But in my heart
She'll always have a place.

I tried to deny my feelings for her,
But I love her still.
And I think I always will.

I tried to block her number and memories,
But I failed to forget
How wonderful she is.

But I tried.

December

The last thing I remember,
Sometime in December
With snow falling around,
Was me all alone … and not another sound.

You had gone away from here,
Here on a winter's night,
Where footprints were covered in white.
No other was in sight to ease my winter plight.

Forget me not, not tonight, nor tomorrow.
I leave me to my sorrow.
Your heart I only borrow.

Sometime in December.

Soldier

I have the fortitude to face my fear,
The courage to see darkness through,
The valor to find my way back to you.

Where you have gone is nowhere I cannot follow.

I'll find you before the sun rises tomorrow.

Private Disgraceful

Don't call yourself a soldier.
You're a drunk,
A drug-addicted fiend.
You would sell out your country in the blink of an eye.
I would rather fight alone than have you here
To disgrace my battlefield with your drugs and beer.

1,000 Roads

The 1,000 roads to where you are
Are none very easy to get so far.
You drove away in your car to the west.
If love is a highway, then my journey has just begun,
Down the 1,000 roads between you and I,
Somewhere beyond the morning sky.

Potential Mess

The potential we all possess can be lost,
Lost when life is a mess;

When we are plotted against by others
Who like us less.

Stress clouds a once clear mind,
It causes us to fall behind.

The unexpected things that appear day to day
Complicate us in many a strange way.

Complicated things for which we all must pay
When life is a mess.

What If I

What if I … what a question.
What if I did this?
What if I did that?
What if I said that I loved you?
What would you have done?

Would you have loved me like the only one?
Lived with me here and had a son?
Kissed one another in the morning?
Made love by candle light at night?
Said we were sorry … if ever we would fight?

Why didn't I say what needed to be said?
I let you go into the unknown alone.
How I suffer now without your kiss.
Without my girl … that I'll always miss.
What if I loved you … the way you loved me?

What if I?

What Can I Say?

What can I say about how I feel inside?
It's an amazing feeling to have someone here,
Someone like you who takes away my every tear.

What can I say about what I see in you?
My lonely days are over; my heart is on the mend.

You are a lover and a friend, my beloved to the end.

What can I say about how much I love you?
You are my beloved for infinite reasons.
I love your kiss, may it last for all seasons.

What can I say about Sammie?
Your love lights my way home to an open door.
You are, to me, worth dying for.

What can I say to finish this poem?
Just that I love you always,
Now and all of my days.

What a Disappointment

What a disappointment it was to my eyes,
To see you were gone.
Left without a word, gone without a good-bye.

What a disappointment it was to my heart,
To be betrayed.
Lied to and fooled by you.

What a disappointment it was to my emotions,
To be unloved.
Loved once, but not anymore.

What a disappointment it was to my lips;
They are not kissed.
They longed for you, deceitful you ... but no more.

What a disappointment it was to my soul,
Lying in agony in sad places.

What a disappointment it was to my everything,

Loved and left, loved and lied to.

You never loved me at all ... what a disappointment.

The Rocky Road to Romance

Don't think me unworthy, pretty eyes.
I know what you need now to quench your cries.
I see your empty life and lies.

Don't think me unworthy, pretty eyes.
You are my dream to dream about.
I can't deny I love you without a doubt.

2005

Lonely me

Lonely me, self deceived, and unperceived;

Compulsive, alone, and unrelieved;

Forgotten and unloved;

Confined to six-feet-under solitude;

Throbbing in self-denial.

Mary, Rose of Scotts

I.

How now I melt in view of you,
Someone so sweet.
Only in dreams could we meet.
I've liked you for the longest time
And time again
Sweet and beautiful Mary, rose of Scotts.

II.

Come undone; come to me on trembling feet.
Don't be afraid to give in time
And time again.
Here alone is a lovely place for love to begin,
Sweet and beautiful Mary, rose of Scotts.

III.

Apart were you and I; I missed your smile
And sweet face.
Where we were was a sad place time and time again.
We found one another beyond vastness
And space,
Sweet and beautiful Mary, rose of Scotts.

IV.

What dreams did you dream
While deep in sleep?
Were they of you and I kissing, loving, and living?
Living a happy life together time
And time again,
Sweet and beautiful Mary, rose of Scotts.

V.

Comes now time to end this rhyme.
How now I weep in view of you.
Unrequited love revealed in tears time and time again,
Sweet and beautiful Mary, rose of Scotts.

Blonde and Bright

Take me away
With arms so tight,
Beautiful angel,
Blonde and bright.

I don't know your name,
You with watchfulness and passion,
Heartbreaking beauty,
Blonde and bright.

Take me away
From all this pain, all this death,
Uncertainty and disdain.

If Lindsey Were My Lover

If Lindsey were my lover,
I would caress her like no other.
There would never be another,
If Lindsey were my lover.

If Lindsey were my lover,
Our passionate embrace could last forever.
Nothing would come between us … ever,
If Lindsey were my lover.

If Lindsey were my lover,
Caress her sweet face, kiss her sweet lips.
Feel her love for me, down to my fingertips,
If Lindsey were my lover.

If Lindsey were my lover,
We would travel the world forever.
See the sights far away together,
If Lindsey were my lover.

If Lindsey were my lover,
She could see my love for her,
And I could kiss her lips and see the love,
The love in Lindsey's eyes,
If Lindsey were my lover.

The Love in Lindsey's Eyes

I see the love in Lindsey's eyes.
I feel Lindsey's sweet touch.
I hold her tight in the darkness of the night,
Our naked bodies wrapped together,
Our hands holding on tight.
The gentle sound of her breathing is comfort,
And it's just right.

I made sweet love to that sweet girl,
And held her tight and found peace in her arms.
I slept there all night.

I love her so much, everything about her.
She's intoxicating to me.
I think of her always when we are apart,
How I combed her hair in the morning light.
She kissed my face, and I knew she loved me.
It was easy to see

The love in Lindsey's eyes.

The Memory of You

The memory of you resonates like a knife;
Cutting me with good memories and bad,
And dreams of love and loss.

The memory of you… alive and dead too,
Your body six feet under.
The memory of you… one thousand feet above.

Nature

Nature is all around,
Every little sound.
Things I cannot see.
A whole world around
More infinite than me.

Merry Travelers

Merry travelers pass in the night.
Most of them never meet,
And tread softly on their traveling feet.

Tomorrow

As long as I live,
There will always be today.
But when I am gone,
There will be no tomorrow.

2006

Untitled

A tragic end to a love that could have been;
The death of romance that never had its chance.

The loss of two people who could have loved;
Loved one another like no other.

No other soul could bare me comfort;
None to soothe my broken heart.

No other to see how much I cared;
No other to see how fiercely I loved.

Where broken hearts go to die;
Where the many lovers come to cry.

This is where my heart will be;
This is the end for you and me.

That is where I will always love you;
That is ocean of time that I have crossed.

When hearts transcend death;
Where love never dies.

From the Start

I loved you from the start,
Green eyes and all heart.

Where love is so grand,
And only we can understand.

The life we could share,
So bright and so fair.

Green eyes and all heart,
I loved you from the start.

Untitled

Take my hand.
Come with me
Where lovers sing.
And tell me what can I do
To make you see
It can only be you and me,
Forever and only,
Endless love or the broken heart.

It's hard to know.
What can I do
To get to you
To make you see
It can only be you and me.

Untitled

The heart still beats
For a lovesick fool
When life is gone.

The love still lives
Inside the heart
Of those he loved.

His life still lives in memory
Of those who still
Are alive.

The heart doesn't die.
Even though we cry,
The heart still beats.

For a lovesick fool,
Once he's loved
He will never stop.

Dance with Me

Dance with me
Through fields of dreams
Where we won't fall.

Where the rain can't come
And darkness dies,
Dance with me.

I still believe in you and me.
It's hard to see a life without you,
Without you inside my beating heart.

Dance with me.
Sing a song.
Let me love you endlessly.

2007

Amplify My Love

Amplify my love.
Augment my sentiment.
Raise my spirit.
Deepen my affection.
Wide my want for you.
Extend your love to encompass me too.

Sometimes

Sometimes all alone,
I feel no trust between us,
Between me and you.
What am I supposed to do?
How can I live this lie?

Sometimes when I cry,
I feel no trust between us.
I was all alone
Until I found you.
What am I supposed to do?

Sometimes when I dream,
I feel no trust between us.
What am I supposed to do,
Go on living without you?
I'll be all alone.

Sometimes though it pains,
I feel no trust between us.
It's impossible.
What am I supposed to do?

White Roses for Pretty Eyes

White roses for pretty eyes,
I came to you.
With white roses for pretty eyes,
Can you see?

Those roses that I bought for you,
Those white roses for pretty eyes,
Dry your lonely tears.
Stand here close to me.

I'll make you see, pretty eyes,
Those white roses that I gave to you.
My heart was in your hands.
My love was in your pretty eyes.

Those white roses
Didn't make you cry.
Dry your lonely tears.
I came to you,
Pretty eyes.

You and Me

Today like the one before me,
You said you weren't free.
What will come of you and me?

Yesterday like the one before me,
We couldn't be.
I'm crying in my hands over you and me.

Tomorrow will be
The saddest day of my life,
Another heartbreak I can see.

In a thousand years
You won't be free.
What became of you and me?

My Karyla Jean

My Karyla Jean,
Your smile is so much brighter
Than my TV screen.
You're so much sweeter than I had seen.

My Karyla Jean,
Take me home.
Your eyes certainly light my way.
I could feel you today.
I could remember you for a million years.

My Karyla Jean,
Your love certainly dried my tears.
Your touch touched my heart.
Your love took me away to somewhere green.

My Karyla Jean,
How can I make you see?
How can I win your heart?
You're tearing mine apart.

My Karyla, My Inamorata

My inamorata,
With hands on my throbbing heart.
Object of my affection,
My sweetheart.
My most precious paramour,
My darling dear whom I adore.
You're lovely.
You're exquisite.
My love above all others,
My Karyla,
My inamorata.

Untitled

I'm lonesome without you,
Gloomy tonight.
Are you missing me?
My amour, are you lonely too?
My most precious love,
Are you lonesome tonight?

Oblivious

He was frail in the face of fear,
Lost in the art of love,
Oblivious to all that's good or bad.

She was fragrant like the white rose,
Mixed in the world of men,
Oblivious to all who would love her.

They were fascinating to one another,
Found in the allure of devotion,
Oblivious to all but their love.

Annexation

Will you annex me to you?
Affix this ring to your finger.
Append with me forever.
Connect your name to mine.
Til death do us part.

Untitled

What a naughty girl:
Off-color and ribald,
Risqué and raunchy,
Lewd and hot.
What a wife I've got.
Not

Untitled

She's my lover,
My companion and my flame.
We have no sexual relations, but I love her.
I love her just the same.

She's my lover,
My delicious and my heart.
We are each other's missing part.

She's my lover,
My same,
The girl who bears my name.

Untitled

You'll feel my passion from your lips to mine.
Your love's the offer I could never decline.
One night stands are all well and good,
But I love only you, like a lover should.

Inamoratas of the Night

Inamoratas of the night,
On the wings of passing angels,
On the corner of the street.

Inamoratas of the night,
Inamoratas in pairs,
Here and gone again.

Always in pairs,
Inamoratas of the night.

Breezy

Blue skies on a breezy day,
Where everything seems to go my way.
I hear birds chirping far away.
The grass is greener as it lay.
The sun hurts my eyes,
So I turn away.
But it's ok.
It's sunny on this bright and breezy day.

My Night with Josie

In her arms I cried
Tears of joy.

Wipe away my tears,
Sweet girl.

I love you right now
And for eternum.

Kissed your sweet lips.
Felt you in love.

Bathed you in bubbles.
Held you so close.

Made love to you right.
Felt you all night.

I love you, Josie,
And you in return.

Breathe you so deep.
Drift off to sleep.

Dream in your arms.
Dream of me, dream of you, and dream of us.

Salute to the Green Grass

Salute to the green grass growing.
Salute to the green grass blowing,
Blowing left and right at the wind's whim.
I find contentment to mow it down.
I drift from place to place,
From dream to dream and back.
While on my mower,
In a rhythm to turning blades,
I am simply not there.
Salute to the green grass growing.
Salute to the green grass blowing
My mind away.

Cowgirl

Mine eyes have never seen such a lovely cowgirl:
Lovely skin,
Hay-colored hair,
Eyes to get lost in.
So lovely she is,
Like winter's first snowflakes;
After a long hot summer,
Like dreams of Christmastime.

Latex Love

I am bonded to you my love,
My body a shelter from the rain.
The intimacy between us is so strong.
I'll keep you safe in dangerous places.
You put me on.
You let me in,
Tonight and then again.

Chimera

My chimera in the dark,
My fata morgana in the light,
A monster stalks my fancy,
My dire, dreadful dream.

Xanadu

Xanadu for you forever,
Forever and always.
Just like a dream,
Waterfalls and white roses.
Xanadu forever it would seem.
Fruit trees growing tall,
Where everyday is fall.
The grass is always green
In Xanadu forever.

Admire Me

Admire me from afar,
I can't cross the river to where you are.
The water has turned red.
The bridge has fallen and the ferryman is dead.

The river flows between you and me.
I can't swim into the river death,
Where the water has turned red.
The bridge above has fallen and the ferryman is dead.

Admire me from afar.

Untitled

The bicycles rolling by,
Shiny wheels,
Shaded faces,
Off and away to unknown places.

Untitled

Pretty eyes
Going far,
Alongside the passing car.
Strange eyes
And distant whispers,
Happy children
And high beams.

Untitled

Every yell,
Every scream,
Haunt me,
Like a terrible fata morgana dream.

Untitled

The night cars and faces keep going by,
Faster and faster.
Keep going,
Faster and faster.
Run, run, run
Until your night's task is done.

Untitled

The ocean's chill is cold.
The waves are many and many more.
The ocean is distant and black as night.

The beach isn't silent;

Empty as a graveyard,
But much louder.

The ocean's chill is cold.

I see no faces in the dark,
But I hear them.

Silence comes,
But only for moments.

Untitled

My hands are frozen
And my lips chapped.

My pen scribbles my ramblings,
As I stand idly in the dark.

I hear screams in the night;
Laughter to the left,
Screams to the right,
And darkness all around.

Untitled

These streets aren't empty,
Lively as could be.

The girl with the cute smile
Was looking at me.

Untitled

She made a U-turn
And came my way.
Blinded by high-beams,
I couldn't see,
Until the girl who was driving
Crashed into me.

Go Away, Misery

Go away, misery.
Take your sorrow.
Take it away
To some other beach,
Away from me.

Bikini Girl

Go back to the sea,
Beautiful bikini girl.
Leave me be.
All from the water they come,
Come to torment me.

Untitled

I'm surrounded by women,
Bikinis and little tops.
I can't stomach the sight
Of women here, such a crop.
I'm so alone.
I'm surrounded by women.
I want one.

Hotter Than Hell

It's hotter than hell
Outside today.
I'd rather sit inside
And bask in the cool air.
I just may.

Belly Button baby

Belly Button baby,
What have I done?
You're so pretty,
Shiny in the sun.

Attraction

I shouldn't be here.
Attraction to flesh
Is dangerous for me.
I'm vulnerable to beauty,
And that is all I see.
My heart is too fragile
To be broken again.
It was an attraction to flesh and bare skin
That nearly did me in.

This and There

All day long going this and there,
Blinded by the heat of the sun,
Swallowed up by a tornado of endless and redundant toil.

Deception

My inamorata deceived me.
Used me and gone.
The last of winter's gifts
Was not yet hers.

So lovely her face;
How I desired her.
So money I gave her
For the promise of time.

My inamorata deceived me.
The money she took
For the last of winter's dreams.
I was not yet hers.

So lovely her face;
How she deceived me.
So in love I felt
But not for the broken promise.

My inamorata deceived me.
Used me and gone.

The Gray Man

The gray man is a thief,
A burglar in not so subtle skin.
Stole my Karyla;
Threatened me if I dare,
Dare talk to her again.

The gray man is unbalanced,
Unsafe and crooked
Like a broken house foundation.
Threaten me he will not, if he dare,
Dare talk to me again.

The gray man watches me
When I enter where he dwells,
Like a gray buzzard circling prey.
Threaten me he will not,
Dare I talk to him.

The gray man stole my Karyla.
Unsafe am I.
Crooked now is he,
Unbalanced on those broken legs.

Freedom Isn't Free

Freedom isn't free.
It's my prerogative, you see,
My boldness and my liberty.

Freedom isn't free.
My unrestraint, my emancipate,
I am unbinded, uncaged, unimpeded.

Freedom isn't free.
I'll do as I will,
Self-governing, self-ruling, separate.

Free

Baby's Butterflies

I gave baby butterflies
With the words I said to her.
I made her heart flutter
And skip a beat or two.

I gave baby butterflies
With the kiss I gave today.

I made her smile bright
And happy for a while, tonight.

I gave baby butterflies,
My baby with her hazel eyes.

I made her see, I made her feel,
And now I've got baby's love.

And baby's got butterflies.

Untitled

How pointless
How vain
How useless
How empty
How sad
How ugly
How brilliant
How exquisitely lonely
How Me

From My Heart to Yours

From my heart to yours,
I feel the love burning inside.
Time after time, deep in my mind,
From my heart to yours.

From my heart to yours,
I see your love growing so strong.
So I'm writing this poem.
I'm singing your song,
From my heart to yours.

From my heart to yours,
I feel our hearts beating so fast.
I can't let go of your sweet memory,
From my heart to yours.

From my heart to yours,
I taste the tender way you love me.
I love the way your sweet heart is true,
From my heart to yours.

From my heart to yours,
I smell the wonderful scent you leave.
This is your poem, baby. This is your song,
From my heart to yours.

Untitled

Beautiful, beautiful, beautiful,
Go on walking by.
Don't look back at me.
It doesn't matter.
You'll never see.

Untitled

Oh, what you do to me, my only one.
You have loved me like no other has done.

You've stolen my heart,
Possessed my mind, taken my sadness … torn it apart.

Now I'm blinded by love… I can't see.
Oh, baby, what you do to me.

Poem for the Lost Lovely

My lost lovely,
Gone too far away.
I can feel your gentle sway
Coming closer everyday.

My lost lovely,
Groveling gains me no ground,
Nor tears or sorrow sound.
One thousand apologies until you come around.

My lost lovely,
Your love means to I
A reason for one not yet to die.
Send me not from your door to cry.

My lost lovely,
Though we be states apart,
Distance can't break a heart.
A love forged in steel from the start.

My lost lovely,
Return to me again.
What a life we could begin.
I'll love you even more then.

My lost lovely,
Gone too far away.
I can feel your gentle sway
Coming closer everyday.

This is your poem, baby, and maybe it's fate that it's lucky number eight.

Untitled

Baby, don't leave me; don't go away.
Love me tonight, love me tomorrow.
To be without your love is to live in sorrow.

Baby, don't hurt me; be careful.
My heart isn't that strong.
But love will never die,
So don't break my heart. Don't make me cry.

Baby, don't forget me.
Remember me in your dreams,
Where I'll always love you.
That's where I'll be.
Don't forget to dream, baby; dream of me.

Damned Familiar Faces

Damned familiar faces in the dark,
Damned familiar faces in the light
I didn't wanna see.
People I once knew,
Now only in memory.

Like a tidal wave
Of heartache comes swiftly,
I didn't wanna see
People I once knew,
Now only in memory.

Damned familiar faces,
Old friends,
Old flames
I didn't wanna see.

Untitled

I'm so angry,
So vicious,
So vengeful.
The gray man flaunts Karyla.
I'm so consumed as too kill.
Like the sun, burning the night,
I've never picked a fight.
Still yet, I'm so angry.

Nemesis

What can a poet do?
With so much anger that's innate,
I've found my nemesis.
And he is the focus of my hate.

Untitled

This is my fate:
To reside alone in shadow
Here amongst strangers,
Where dangers abound
And buzzards circle around.

Waiting

I'm still waiting
After twenty-one years.
I'm still waiting
Here on the sidewalk,
Amongst strangers,
Beneath the white horizon.
The far behind is shades of pink
Stretching across an empty lot.
Of all the loves and all the pain,
So strange it is to be here,
Here on the sidewalk
Amongst strangers.

Lovely Who Lit My Fire

Lovely who lit my fire,
Unquenchable drive and desire,
But also dire hatred for another.
Where is the bastard?
I'm sorry to be so angry.
I'm soothed by her.
The object of my desire,
Lovely who lit my fire.

Brandon versus Brandon

The bastard comes
To ruin my night,
My enjoyment,
My delight.
The moment approaches
When Brandon's will be tested,
And one will be bested.

Night Comes

The night comes over my day,
Spent in tedious preparation
For the evening event to come.
All to be disappointed,
I was ever so close.

Unmended Wounds

Some wounds can never be mended.
Here in a crowded theater,
I am alone, a heart left untended.
And I can never leave.
Above the silence
To deaf ears
Rain my moans and screams.

Sensitive Weeper

I'm a sensitive soul.
But my heart bares scars
That will never mend.
I've buried my sorrow in my work,
Yet there is no poetry stitch
To mend scars so deep,
Scars beneath the surface.
So in my seclusion,
I'll weep.

Forever Karyla Jean

She is forever Karyla Jean.
Should I take her away,
Far away from here?
No … she smiles.
Perhaps she belongs?
She's not mine today,
But she is forever Karyla Jean.

Soda-Pop Tears

Tears of soda pop
Stream my sad face.
In the theater she sits but not with me.
I weep tears of sorrow
Over the music and voices,
And tears of soda pop
Stream down my face.

Untitled

Her smile at him,
A dagger to me,
An insurmountable pain.
And from the crowded movie theater,
I cannot flee.

Color Me Miserable

It is the poet's destined path to find such misery,
To suffer for his art
Like a story.
He is a player with an unknown part.

He has lost more than most,
Suffered and sinned.
A heart broke apart,
All suffering for his art.

A destiny unchosen,
Such misery,
Such pain,
So color me miserable.

Lovely Lindsey

Lovely Lindsey,
How she shines,
Radiates, and emotes.
She's lovely as heaven,
Lovely Lindsey.

Sour Kisses

Love has lost its flavor.
Every kiss I was to savor
Has soured
Like rotten fruit.

Dog of War

I am a dog of war.
I sniff the enemy out.
And bite them as I do my tail,
Furiously and with rage.

Untitled

Give me one more night to change your mind,
One more look to lift your heart,
One more touch to save your life.
Give me one more night to change your mind.

Give me one more kiss to curl your toes,
One more word to lift you up,
One more caress to take your heart.
Give me one more night to change your mind.

Give me one more night to love you, dear,
One more happy tear,
One more love to call my own.
Give me one more night to change your mind.

Give me one more night ...before you say good-bye.

2008

Untitled

My body aches.
My chest hurts.
My tired eyes can see.
My apathy is killing me.

Desperate

I'm desperate for what I cannot touch,
What I cannot smell,
What I cannot have,
What I cannot love.
I'm desperate.
I'm in hell.

Untitled

I need to see her,
Hear her.
Because I love her so much.
I am alone without her touch in a dark place,
Until I see her again
And kiss her sweet face.

Pancake Love

Behind her table,
Behind her chair,
Behind this couch,
Way over there.
Short stack, baby,
Pancake love.

Untitled

A million eyes can't fill my empty.
A thousand smiles can't mask my sorrow.
A hundred girls' voices can't lift me up.
Can't save me from this prison
That I'll live in again tomorrow.

Untitled

Climbing my wall,
Scaling your balcony,
All to reach you,
My one and only all.

Untitled

So lonely
So alone
So empty
So me

Dried out dreams

My dreams are drying up.
My hopes are going down.
My life is falling apart.
A soul shattered,
Like my heart.

Where's Baby?

Where's baby when she's needed?
Love when life wants free to be unheeded.
A heart broken apart needs you to be true.

Where's baby when I want her?
Someone sweet to be complete, a heart that's whole
To fix my soul.
A kiss that I am gonna miss.
A touch so real,
So hungry to feel.

When's baby coming back?
To relight my soul, illuminate the black,
Shine the light of love. When's baby coming back?

The Girl in the Band Room

Purloined glances,
That's what it was.
The way she looked my way;
The way I looked hers.
That's what it was.
Purloined glances,
Nothing more.

Nymphomania Nightmare

Monday
Baby's beating down my door.
Took advantage of me on my floor.
Tuesday
Baby wanted me, oh so bad.
It was fun, I'm not mad.
Wednesday
Baby wanted it here and there.
She got it everywhere.
Thursday
Baby likes it by the light of the moon.
She even likes it in the afternoon.
Friday
Baby needs it Friday night.
She's my sun, my stars, my moon.

But if baby doesn't stop ... I'll be dead soon.

Point Me Somewhere Pleasant

Point me somewhere pleasant,
Somewhere fun,
Somewhere warm under the sun.

Take me there,
Somewhere nice.
Take me to my own piece of paradise.

The sky belongs to the stars.
The road belongs to me.
I belong to you.

Point me somewhere pleasant,
Somewhere quiet,
Where I can see a tree.

Take me there,
Somewhere far away.
Take me home, sweet girl.

The sea belongs to the lost,
The heart to the loved,
And we to each other.

Untitled

Idiosyncratic man,
That's what I am.

Wounded deeply by the thorns of life,
Living in lonely solace.

Precariously neurotic,
That's what I am.

Idiosyncratic man

Who's Mr. Heavy Foot?

Who's Mr. Heavy Foot?
Who's heavy on the gas?
Who drives like a maniac?
Who passes every car?
Who's Mr. Heavy Foot?
You are.

Mariachi Man

A diamond-covered charro star,
With a wide colorful sombrero,
I don't understand a word you're saying.
But I dig your guitar,
And I really like your playing.

Untitled

I can't see.
Find me here and there.
I'll be yours; find me somewhere.
Let it be.
Let it be me.

In Stephanie Lynn

In Stephanie Lynn,
Once I was there.
Now will never be again.

In Stephanie Lynn,
I felt tranquil.
In dreams, every now and then…

I'm back, back in Stephanie Lynn.

Hands

Holding hands,
Crossing the street;
Look at her smile.
Isn't it neat?

Holding hands,
Up the steps;
Look at her face.
Isn't it sweet?

Holding hands,
Down the sidewalk;
Look at their love.
Aren't they complete?

Kiss My Asphalt

Look at this lot:
Gray asphalt,
Wet and dirty ground.

Look at my spot.
I'm parked here everyday,
The same old lot.

Look at my life:
The same old car,
The same old, faded scar.

Look at this lot:
Black and cracked asphalt,
The same old me.

The same old empty,
Lonely me,
Alone and forgot.

Untitled

Going down,
Down to dwell in the dark.

Going down,
The water covers me over.

Going down,
Down to sleep in the deep.

Going down,
The water so black.

Going down,
Down and I'm not coming back.

Going down,
Baring heavy feet.

Going down,
Down to the deep, dark … to drown.

Brandon's Song

Here we go again,
Along where I have always been.
The same car,
The same empty dreams of another world,
Another world that's too far.

Remember Me

Remember me, Stephanie Lynn.
When I kissed you ... and the dead lay near.

Remember me, Samantha Joe.
When I loved ... and let you go.

Remember me, Karyla Jean.
When I came to you ... baring white roses.

Haunted hearts aren't enough.

Remember me.
Remember all that stuff.

Untitled

If we can fill this distance between us,
Baby, we can love ... baby, we can be ... together.
I'll take you places you've never been.

If we can find the words to say what we feel,
Baby, we can have all our dreams be real.
I'll make love to you and the darkness will be light.

If we can be together, we'll always be free.
Baby, we can drive to places unknown, somewhere we have never been.
I'll take you away from your pain and your anger.

If we can make love and watch the sunrise,
Baby, I'll love you until the last breath in me ... dies.
I'll make you happy; life will be ours for living.

Life will be ours,
If we can be together.

Untitled

I have music.
I have shoes.
I have clothes.
I have air.

I got no reason to be so blue.
But, baby, I don't have you.

I don't have you
To sing goodnight.

I don't have you.
I don't feel alright.

If I don't have you,
I won't last the night.

If I don't have you,
Baby, if I don't have you,

I'm through.

Montgomery Mountains and Me

Out the window is beautiful, I can see
The streets of Montgomery, WV.

Across the tracks,
And over the roofs,

Beyond the river,
Above the road,

Beneath a white sky,
Lay mountains white with snow.

Back to the road,
And beyond the river,

Over the rooftops,
And across the tracks,

Above the city streets of Montgomery, WV,
In the window is nothing fancy … just me.

Pedestrian

It's not pedestrian to be so broken,
To have fallen so far
And ache for touch,
To dream of impossible, incandescent love so much.
Craving sustenance in desire, a heart set on fire.

It's not pedestrian to be so obscure,
To be so cryptic,
Panglossian in the ways of love,
To dream of a celestial girl
Perfunctory to all else.

It's not pedestrian to be me.

Untitled

It's always the same story,
When the prettiest girl you dated
Leaves you all alone.

Why did you leave me, Stephanie Lynn?

It's in our nature to grieve,
Too suffer.

Oh, Stephanie Lynn,
How I miss you.

Oh god, baby,
How I need you here.

Stephanie Lynn,
So lovely,
So gone.

Untitled

My dearest baby doll,
Angel with green eyes,
Gave to me all.

Whom fate and life took away,
So I am reminded everyday
Over the scent of sorrow and of liquor.

I've tried to drink you away,
But your memory won't go.
So again … hello.

It's good to see you again.
How have you been?
You're always in my mind.

Your face,
Your voice,
Your fingertips,
Your kiss so sweet … liquor on my lips.

Untitled

I want her back.
How I suffer now without her.
Without my Sammie,
I am empty,
Like a bucket turned over.

Tears for Sammie

Tears for Sammie;
I miss her, here and then gone.
I cry.
I weep.
I shed tears for my Sammie,
Here and then gone.

Untitled

Don't go without me, love,
Into the unknown.
Don't go without me, love,
Alone.

Untitled

If I could only hear your voice,
I could leave my heart.
Lest I hear nothing,
And it be ripped apart.

Love Has Come and Gone

My love has gone, gone away.
Someday she'll be back.
She'll come again one day.
Come home with me to stay.

Untitled

In the shadow of my dreams,
Love again one day will return.
And Sammie comes to take me away.

I Pray

I pray to be reunited with my love so far away.
She was here.
I wouldn't let her stay.
I pray to be reunited with my love so far away.
Lest I be alone forever,
Each and every day.

Tears of Blood

I weep tears of blood for Sammie.
Her love washed away.
Please, God, bring her back to me today.

Untitled

I can taste you, baby,
So sweet ... so soft.
But it's only a dream.
Your love is lost.

Piggy

Come home to me, angel.
Come back.
My piggy's love has left,
Left my life so empty,
Alone and bereft.
My piggy with skin that pulled me in;
A touch so warm and gentle,
A body so caressable,
A tummy so kissable,
Passion so intense.
A piggy that's ticklish under the midnight covers.

Where is My Sammie Angel?

Where is my Sammie Angel?
Why isn't she here?
Where did she go?
Why did I leave her?
Was I lonely out of fear?
Where is my Sammie Angel?

No More Stars

There is no more love for me.
Like stars in the sky,
Unreachable, far away,
No more love for me today.

Going Home

I'm going home lonely.
I'm going home sad.
I'm going home without you.
And that's too bad.

Untitled

Like autumn emptiness,
Leaves lay around.
Emptiness for Brandon,
Unhappiness abound.

Untitled

No pretty face to my right.
No hands to my left.
No kisses to my lips.
No love in sight.

Misery

Profound misery, misery, misery.
No happiness in sight.
No joy for me around.
Misery is what I've found.
Profound misery, misery, misery.

Untitled

Bottle my sorrow.
Take it all.
More will come tomorrow.

Untitled

Will today never end?
Will joy not find thee?
Put thee on the mend.

Endless Beauty

In endless, never-ceasing beauty,
Walking right good-bye,
I saw paradise.
It didn't even say hello.

Untitled

How much misery must I endure?
When will she come
And unlock my door?

Take Notice

Why won't she see?
What can I do,
So she'll notice me?

My Eternal Fiancée

Off they go, to another place,
While I stay here
To grieve for her.
Her whose lovely face
I may never see again.
She was mine for a time,
Now gone away,
My eternal fiancée.

Untitled

Cursed clouds
Empty looks
Death shrouds
Endless books

The Man from Misery Returns

Came again,
The man from sorrow sprung.
Baring unrequited love,
Sad songs yet to be sung.
A lonely and sad soul,
The man from sorrow sprung,
Came again.

Boozy Tide

Drown my sorrow in a tide of booze,
Lose myself, my soul, my sanity.
Without you, living is vanity.
So drown my sorrow in a tide of booze,
Till it returns tomorrow.

Truth Lies

She has a boyfriend.
She's got a guy.
That's alright.
The truth is better than a lie.

Foot Beat

Can you hear it?
The beat of passing feet,
The melody of misery,
The song of sorrow
Passes by my street,
The beat of passing feet.

Black and White Light

I'm in the dark,
Standing in the light.
Shrouded in black,
Dressed all in white.

Untitled

Melancholy and miserable,
Lonely and undesirable,
Empty and indescribable,
BRANDON.

Blind

I can't see you anymore
Behind this big door.
Open up,
Lest you leave me
Dying on the floor.

Untitled

If fate swept me away,
Here it came,
Gone today.
If fate swept me away,
Here I'll be,
In your heart to stay.

I'm Holding Sorrow

I'm holding sorrow in love's embrace.
Every time I want you,
You're some other place.
I'm holding sorrow in love's embrace.

2009

2009

I'm fishing for more knowledge than I know what to do.
It's all over the place, coming faster than I can process it.
I'm drowning in a sea of books and dates and stories,
In random bits of information that seem to cling to me,
Cling to me like skin.

Am I Poe?

Am I Poe,
Doomed to a life of sorrow and woe?
I don't know.

Somebody

I will be somebody someday.
You'll see.
But first and most important,
I will be ME.

After Death

I feel better
After a week under the weather.
I feel better
Having been near death.
I've never felt so alive.

Salute to '09

This be the year of Poe,
The birth of Lincoln,
The saga of Barack,
Salute to you, '09.

Thank You

I'll be
Your love, and you'll know.
Without you
I would be lost.
You take me
Places I can't go.
And I thank you so much, baby.

Smarter Than This

I wish I could be
Smarter than this.
I wish I could see
What I know I will miss.
I wish I could be
Smarter than this.

Untalented Dreamer

Am I
Untalented dreamer?
Mind flying, left behind,
Melancholy schemer.
Am I
Untalented dreamer?
Left flying,
Mind behind and crying.
I am
Or am I
Untalented dreamer?

Unattainable

Beauty unattainable,
I cannot touch.
She's so close.
I need her so much,
Unattainable beauty.

Swallowed Up

In her eyes I see my dreams.
Swallowed by her soul,
I can't get them back
From her eyes.

Mystery

What's her name?
She's so close to me,
Yet such a mystery.
What's her dream?
Let her be.
Yet she's so close to me
She's a mystery.

Pillows

Soft silk and sugar
Across her chest.
Wonderful pillows,
So warm, so soft
Her breasts.

Salute to Jessy

Hey, cutie,
Are you still engaged
Or are you wed?
I hope it's the former,
Lest I have a chance
To ponder your beauty.

Jessy

So silent,
So sweet,
So mysterious,
Yet upbeat.
In a sea of strangers,
She's above the surface
Like light glistening on ripples.

Death

Death for me
Comes and goes,
Like an endless swinging pendulum,
Ever back and forth.

Shower Duet

In that room
Just behind a closed door,
She showers alone.
If only she knew what's in my heart,
She would shower me with love and bubbles.
In each others arms,
A shower duet.

Back in Time

Oh, god,
I'm going back to last year.
I'm shaking.
I'm repeating.
I'm seeing.
It's happening again.
I'm going back.
Oh, god,
It must be fate.
I'm going back in time,
Back to '08.

Chilled

My hands are shaking.
Is it the cold
Or something other?
Deep in my soul
To the core I am chilled,
Pale and old.

Papaw

What would I ask of papaw
Were he here today?
Was he beaten in the mine,
A small and helpless child?
Why did he return
To the mine so dark?
Did he not aspire to be something more?
Papaw what can I do
To be like you?

Help Me, Edgar

Help me, Edgar.
My work's so misunderstood.

Help me, Edgar,
To be loved like I should.

Help me, Edgar,
For my words to make sense.

Help me, Edgar.
What can I do?

Help me, Edgar,
To be like you.

Untitled

Her face changes at every new glance.
She's my inspiration,
My melancholy romance.

A Poet's Love

Never reveal your work,
For they'll not understand.
It takes a poet's touch
To love a poem this much.

Untitled

I'm better than them,
You'll see.
I'm a better poet
Then they'll ever be.

Untitled

Words can't escape from my pen and page.
I know the way
To take them apart,
To write a poem of the heart.

Untitled

My poems are the voice that I do not have.
If I write loud enough
Perhaps she will hear.
Maybe she'll come
Save me from fear.

Destiny

I am destined for good or bad,
To dress in black and never come back,
To walk in light in the darkest night.
I am destined for happy or sad,
To be happy for being alive,
To be sad for losing what I had.

I am destined for what ... I cannot say.

Untitled

This isn't where I belong,
In here.
It feels wrong.
It isn't like they'll come and say,
Hey, are you okay?
Not today.
This isn't where I belong.

Untitled

Why do they ignore me?
Leave me be.
Can't they see?

Hatred

I hate their smiles,
Their denials,
Their happiness and wiles.
I hate them to the core of my soul
For the life they stole,
For all their happiness and love.
I hate them
From below and above.

French Fried Rage

I am turned green
By the lifting smell of fries.
I am red with rage
For the happy in their eyes.

Life's Song

I've tried to ignore
Life's sad and sorrowful song.
But I can't,
Not anymore.

Laughter of Many Clowns

It's driving me mad,
Their laughter in my head.
It sounds so bad.
I wish I were dead.

Untitled

If I could run,
Sprint out the door,
I would be done,
Brandon, no more.

Some Angel

They come.
They go.
Girls, girls, girls,
I don't know their names.
But I'll know the one for me.
She'll be there.
You'll see.

Untitled

Women make no sense to me.
They are at best ... a mystery.

Untitled

Baby girl is so pretty.
What can I do?
She's such a beauty.
God, help me.
Baby's scent is in the air.
It's not fair.

Untitled

I wish I could forget
The story I just heard.
I wish I could forget it,
Every single word.

About Terrorists

Terrorists come
Knockin' on our door.
They wanna challenge us.
We'll give 'em a war.

Untitled

I didn't know
What to say,
What to do.
I don't have any idea
How to talk to you.

Music Man

I had an epiphany
Just yesterday.
What if I were a man of music?
What if I could play?

Chimerical Dream

My clandestine angel
Of the darkest nature
Was to me everything.
With a love so deep,
I did not return from it.
I am there,
Lost in a chimerical dream
Where she is with me.
My clandestine angel,
The white lights of her eyes shine
And bring tears to mine.

Untitled

If I were a biker
Riding the highways black,
I'd be a ghost, never to come back.

If I were a farmer
Plowing my fields all day,
I'd be just a whisper on the wind, blown away.

If I were a soldier
Baring a gun in my hand,
I'd be just a voice from the past, haunting the land.

If I were someone's lover
Holding her tight in my embrace,
I'd be just her man,

Her world's most recognizable face.